W9-CHX-755

Walt Disney

Published in the United States of America by Cherry Lake Publishing
Ann Arbor, Michigan
www.cherrylakepublishing.com

Content Adviser: Ryan Emery Hughes, Doctoral Student, School of Education, University of Michigan
Reading Adviser: Marla Conn MS, Ed., Literacy specialist, Read-Ability, Inc.
Book Design: Jennifer Wahi
Illustrator: Jeff Bane

Photo Credits: © Bill Grant / Alamy Stock Photo, 5; © Moviestore collection Ltd / Alamy Stock Photo, 7; © U.S. Information Agency/National Archives and Records Association, 9, 22; © Ronald Grant Archive / Alamy Stock Photo, 11; © Moviestore collection Ltd / Alamy Stock Photo, 13; © AF archive / Alamy Stock Photo, 15; © Carol M. Highsmith/Library of Congress, 17, 23; © Glasshouse Images / Alamy Stock Photo, 19; © Pictorial Press Ltd / Alamy Stock Photo, 21; Cover, 8, 12, 16, Jeff Bane; Various frames throughout, Shutterstock Images

Library of Congress Cataloging-in-Publication Data

Names: Haldy, Emma E., author.
Title: Walt Disney.
Description: Ann Arbor : Cherry Lake Publishing, 2016. | Series: My
   itty-bitty bio | Includes bibliographical references and index.
Identifiers: LCCN 2015045609| ISBN 9781634710244 (hardcover) | ISBN
   9781634711234 (pdf) | ISBN 9781634712224 (pbk.) | ISBN 9781634713214
   (ebook)
Subjects: LCSH: Disney, Walt, 1901-1966--Juvenile literature. |
   Animators--United States--Biography--Juvenile literature.
Classification: LCC NC1766.U52 D5426 2016 | DDC 741.58092--dc23
LC record available at http://lccn.loc.gov/2015045609

Printed in the United States of America
Corporate Graphics

About the author: Emma E. Haldy is a former librarian and a proud Michigander. She lives with her husband, Joe, and an ever-growing collection of books.

About the illustrator: Jeff Bane and his two business partners own a studio along the American River in Folsom, California, home of the 1849 Gold Rush. When Jeff's not sketching or illustrating for clients, he's either swimming or kayaking in the river to relax.

I was born in 1901. I grew up in Missouri.

I was playful. I loved to draw.

I worked as an artist. But I had bigger dreams.

I opened an **animation studio**. My brother helped me.

What would you like to do when you grow up?

I created a character. I called him Mickey Mouse.

I made a cartoon with Mickey.
It was called *Steamboat Willie*.

The cartoon was special.
It had sound! That was new
technology. It paid off.
Mickey was a hit!

I kept working. I had more ideas.
I wanted to make animated
movies.

I made *Snow White and the Seven Dwarfs*. It was **artistic**. It was beautiful.

Nothing like it had ever been done before. People loved it.

I kept making movies. I started making television shows.

I became famous. Children loved me. They called me Uncle Walt.

What is your favorite Disney movie?

I imagined a place for families
to have fun together. I built a
theme park, Disneyland.

It was magical! I was very proud.

I took a special interest in the book *Mary Poppins*. I liked that it was about family.

I made it into a movie. People said it was my best. It was a great success.

I was working on plans for another park. But I got sick.
I died at age 65.

I was a creative man. I brought fun and joy to children.
I reminded people to imagine.

What would you like to ask me?

1928

1900

Born
1901

1955

2000

Died
1966

glossary

animation (an-uh-MAY-shuhn) creating drawings, pictures, or computer graphics to make movies

artistic (ahr-TIS-tik) able to create things using imagination

studio (STOO-dee-oh) a place where movies, television and radio shows, or recordings are made

technology (tek-NAH-luh-jee) the use of science and engineering to make things better

index